Ike and Mike

by Maria Fleming
illustrated by Kelly Kennedy

SCHOLASTIC INC.

New York • Toronto • London • Auckland • Sydney
Mexico City • New Delhi • Hong Kong • Buenos Aires

Designed by Maria Lilja
ISBN-13: 978-0-439-88459-4 • ISBN-10: 0-439-88459-4
Copyright © 2006 by Scholastic Inc.
All rights reserved. Printed in the U.S.A.

First printing, November 2006

12 11 10 9 8 7 6 5   9 10 11/0

This is **Ike**. This is **Ike's** brother, **Mike**.

Ike does not like to share with Mike.
Mike does not like to share with Ike.

Ike has a new **white bike**.
"Can **I ride** your **bike**?" **Mike** asks **Ike**.
"No way!" says **Ike**. "It's **mine**!"

Mike likes to **fly** his **kite** in the **sky**.

"Can **I try** to **fly** your **kite**?" **Ike** asks **Mike**.

"No **way**!" says **Mike**. "It's **mine**!"

It would be **fine** to **dine** here.

RISE AND SHINE DINER

Today's Specials
• Slice of Pizza
• Rice and Beans
• Spice Cake with Ice Cream

Phonics Fact

The vowel pair *ie* can also make the long-*i* sound, as in **fries**. Can you find another long-*i* word with the same spelling pattern on this page?

(Answer: **pie**)

At **lunchtime, Ike** has French **fries**. **Mike** has **lime pie**.

"Can **I try a fry**?" **Mike** asks **Ike**.

"No way!" says **Ike**. "It's **mine**! Can **I try** a **bite** of **pie**?"

"No way!" says **Mike**. "It's **mine**!"

Ike and **Mike spy** a toy. They each have **five dimes**. Will they share their **dimes** to get the toy? No way!

Phonics Fact

Another spelling pattern that makes the long-*i* sound is *igh*, as in **fight**. Other words with this pattern are **sigh**, **might**, and **right**. Be on the lookout for more!

Ike and **Mike** begin to **fight**.

Then **Ike** and **Mike** begin to **cry**. A **wise fly** buzzes **by**.

"Boys, take **my advice**," he says with a **sigh**. "It's **nice** to share."

"That **fly might** just be **right**," says **Ike**.
"Let's give it a **try**," says **Mike**.

Ike and **Mike** think sharing is **mighty fine**!

That **night**, **Ike** shares his book of **rhymes** with **Mike**. **Mike** shares his stuffed **lion**, **Spike**, with **Ike**.

The **fly smiles** with **delight** as he turns out the **light**. "What a **sight**! Sleep **tight**! Good **night**!"

Long-i Riddles

Listen to the riddles. Then match each riddle with the right long-*i* word from the box.

> **Word Box**
> fly   dime   bite   smile   pie
> hi   wise   lime   bike   night

1 You do this when you are happy.

2 This is something you eat for dessert.

3 You can buy things with this coin.

4 This is a bug.

5 This has wheels and you can ride it.

6 It means *smart*.

7 It is the opposite of *day*.

8 This green fruit tastes sour.

9 It means the same thing as *hello*.

10 You do this when you eat an apple.

Long-i Cheer

Hooray for long *i*, the best sound around!

Let's holler long-*i* words all over town!

There's **like** and **nice** and **bike** and **kite**.

There's **fly** and **sky** and **light** and **night**.

There's **pie** and **my** and **five** and **find**.

There's **write** and **rice** and **size** and **kind**.

Long *i*, long *i*, give a great cheer

For the **finest** sound you ever will hear!

Make a list of other long-*i* words. Then use them in your cheer.